Diet recommendations for TCM - Large intestine - Moist heat in the colon

Please check these recommendations always with a TCM nutrition consultant, therapist, doctor or dietician. The recipes and the list of ingredients are supporting also the conventional medical therapy. The calorie disclosures of fresh ingredients (fruit and vegetables) vary according to quality and time of harvest. The contents were checked by a dietician and a nutrition consultant for the Traditional Chinese Medicine (TCM).

Author:
©2017 Josef Miligui
www.ebns.at

AF236088

Source:
The lists are created from the EBNS database for nutritional counseling. The database is used by dietitians, therapists and doctors for advising the patient / client.

Literature:
The specialist literature and the training documents of the German and Austrian dietary and traditional Chinese medicine serve as a knowledge base. We have used the documents as a basis of knowledge, adapted it to our experience and completed them.
http://di-book.com

Title Photo:
©2008 Erika Weixlbaumer

Production and publishing:
BoD – Books on Demand, Norderstedt
ISBN: 9783752861495

Diet recommendations for TCM - Large intestine - Moist heat in the colon

1 Treatment strategy

Stop diarrhea, cool the heat, remove moisture.

2 Avoid

n.a.

3 Breakfast

	kkal. per serving
Adzuki Bean and Rice Soup	199
Apple - banana cream	110
Colorful tuscan bean soup	249
Cream cheese substitute	526
Fish soup with rosemary	271

7 Dinner

8 Any time

9 Recipes

(recommendable) = You can use more.
(little) = You should use less than specified or omit.

9.1 8 treasures of rice

Strengthens kidney and bladder, builds up Qi, strengthens the spleen, repels moisture, reduces internal heat, prevents cancer, builds heart, calms nerves.
Cooking time approx. 1 hour
Calories p. portion: 212
4 portions

Quantity of ingredients
Lily bulbs 1 table spoon / 5g. (recommended)....................................*
Longane 1 table spoon / 5g. (recommended).....................................*
King Solomon's-seal 1 table spoon / 5g. (recommended)..................*
Yam root, yam root tuber 1 table spoon / 5g. (recommended)...........*
Coix (seeds) YiYi Ren 1 table spoon / 5g. (recommended) ....*
Rice wild (nature rice) 1 1/2 cups / 240g. (recommended)..........metal
Water 8-10 cups / 800g. (yes) .... earth

Cooking instructions:
Each one 1 tbsp: Bai He, Longan, Yu Zhu, Da Zao, Shan Yao, Lian Mi, Yi Yi Ren, Qian Shi
Add hot water and soak for about 30 minutes. Then add 1 - 2 cups of rice (normal) and simmer for 1/2 to 1 hour until the rice is very soft. Or: Cook for about 3 hours with the herbs a congee. Then the herbs do not have to be soaked.

9.2 Adzuki Bean and Rice Soup

Reduces moisture, directs down, reduces gastrointestinal heat, builds up essence, strengthens muscles after heat illness, builds up body fluids.
Cooking time approx. 2 hours
Calories p. portion: 199
1 portions
Quantity of ingredients
Adzuki beans 8 table spoons / 40g. (recommended)..................water
Rice round grain 2 table spoons / 20g. (recommended).............metal
Water 1 1/2 cups / 200g. (yes)... earth
Honey 1 table spoon / 8g. (recommended) .... earth

Cooking instructions:
Boil soaked adzuki beans and round grain rice in a ratio of 4: 1 in water until a thin pulp has formed. Sweet as needed; possibly puree.

Effect: This recipe strengthens kidney, spleen and stomach and is particularly suitable for mothers with too little milk flow.

9.3   Apple - banana cream

Protects the fluids, reduces internal heat in Yin deficiency, cools heat in the intestine.
Cooking time approx. 15 min
Calories p. portion: 110
4 portions
Quantity of ingredients
Apple (sour) 7/8 lbs / 400g. (recommended)..............................wood
Water 3/4 cup - 6 oz / 200g. (yes)...earth
Orange peel 1/4 piece / 5g. (recommended).....................................*
Lemon peel 1/2 piece / 2g. (recommended)................................. fire
Sugar brown 2 teaspoons / 6g. (recommended) .... earth
Cinnamon sticks 1 piece / 0g. (recommended) ....*
Banana 1 piece / 150g. (recommended)..................................... earth
Acerola fruit nectar or powder 1 teaspoon / 2g. (recommended) wood
Orange juice 1/2 piece / 50g. (recommended) ....wood
Lemon juice 1 table spoon / 10g. (recommended) ....wood

Cooking instructions:
Cut the apple into fine slices, bring water to boil and add the apple slices, orange- and lemon peel, sugar and cinnamon and simmer about 7 minutes. The apples should be almost soft. Remove acerola and the cinnamon stick. Mix the apple, the banana, the orange juice and the lemon juice.

9.4   Asparagus and herb ragout

Nourishes Yin from lung kidney blood and liver, produces humors, feeds Yin, moisturizes, relaxes, builds up Qi, spreads, strengthens spleen and liver, regulates Qi flow.
Cooking time approx. 30 min
Calories p. portion: 168
4 portions
Allergens: GL

Quantity of ingredients
Basic recipe for a vegetable soup 2 cups / 500g. (recommended)......*
Lemon peel 1/2 piece / 3g. (recommended).................................. fire
Coriander 1/4 teaspoon / 1g. (recommended)...........................metal
Nutmeg 1 pinch / 0,3g. (recommended)....................................metal
Asparagus (green or white) 1,8 lbs / 800g. (recommended)....... earth
Parsley 1 Bunch / 125g. (recommended)..................................wood
Créme fraiche cheese 2 table spoons / 30g. (recommended) ....*
Lemon juice 1 teaspoon / 3g. (recommended)..........................wood
Potato 7/8 lbs / 400g. (recommended)..................................... earth

Cooking instructions:
Cook potatoes with plenty of salted water about 20 min. until soft.
Heat the vegetable stock with lemon zest, coriander and nutmeg till it
boil. Cook the peeled and sliced asparagus in it.
Drain asparagus in a sieve. Collect the cooking liquid.
In the blender mix 200 g of cooked asparagus (the lower ends), cooking
liquid and parsley to a smooth sauce. Beat the sauce with crème
fraîche until smooth. Add asparagus and heat again and season with
lemon juice, salt and pepper. Serve with the potatoes.

9.5 Asparagus Cream Soup

Nourishes Yin from lung and kidney, produces humors, feeds Yin,
moisturizes, relaxes, builds up Qi, spreads. moisturizes, laxative,
antiparasitic, nourishes blood and liver, harmonizes liver and spleen,
nourishes Yin from heart and kidney.
Cooking time approx. 45 min
Calories p. portion: 240
2 portions
Allergens: ACG

Quantity of ingredients
Asparagus (green or white) 5/8 oz / 200g. (recommended)........ earth
Water 2 cup / 500g. (yes).. earth
Rapeseed oil 2 table spoons / 30g. (recommended).................. earth
Wheat flour 2 table spoons / 10g. (recommended).....................wood
Chicken yolk 1 piece / 25g. (recommended).............................. earth
Cow's milk (whole 3.5% fat) 1 table spoon / 15g. (recommended).....*
Sour cream 15% fat 1 table spoon / 15g. (recommended)................*
Pepper (ground) 1 pinch / 0,5g. (recommended).......................metal
Nutmeg 1 pinch / 0,5g. (recommended)....................................metal
Lemon juice 1 teaspoon / 2g. (recommended)...........................wood

Parsley 2 table spoons / 20g. (recommended)...........................wood
Salt 1 pinch / 1g. (recommended)...water

Cooking instructions:
Wash and peel the asparagus.
Heat water, a little lemon juice and pinch of salt till it boils. Tie the asparagus spears together.
Add the asparagus peel to the cooking water and bring to the boil.
Add the asparagus and cook on low heat for about 20 minutes.
Then remove the asparagus bunches and pour the broth through a sieve.
For the roux, heat the oil in a saucepan, add the flour and sauté until it is colorless, slowly top up with the asparagus sauce and simmer for 10 minutes. Cut the asparagus spears into pieces about 3 cm long and place them to the soup. Just before serving, bring the soup to the boil again. Mix the egg yolk with the milk and sour cream.
Remove the pot from the heat and stir in the egg yolk and milk mixture. Season with pepper and nutmeg, decorate with the chopped parsley and serve immediately.

9.6   Basic recipe for a vegetable soup, nutritious

Strengthens spleen and lung, regulates Qi flow, builds up Qi, dries out, passes downwardly, strengthens stomach Qi.
Cooking time approx. 2-3 hours
Calories p. portion: 48
5 portions
Allergens: L

Quantity of ingredients
Olive oil 1 table spoon / 4g. (little)...earth
Onion white 1 piece / 60g. (yes) ....metal
Carrot 3 pieces / 200g. (recommended)......................................earth
Parsnip 3/8 lbs - 6oz / 150g. (recommended) .... fire
Celery root 1 cup / 100g. (recommended)...................................earth
Ginger fresh 1/2 teaspoon / 2g. (little)..metal
Lemon 1/2 piece / 25g. ()...wood
Juniper berry 6 pieces / 6g. (recommended)............................... fire
Thyme dried 1 pinch / 1g. (recommended) ....metal
Lovage 1 table spoon / 3g. (recommended)..................................metal
Bay leaf 2 leaves / 1g. (recommended) ....*
Salt 1 pinch / 1g. (recommended)..water
Water 3 cups / 650g. (yes) .... earth

Cooking instructions:
Cut the vegetables into cubes.
Heat oil in hot pot, fry shortly onions and vegetables.
Add cold water, then add ginger, bay leaf and lemon juice.
Season with juniper, thyme and lovage. Cover for 2 - 3 hours on a low heat and simmer.
The used vegetables should be thrown away.
The basic recipe serves as a soup base and to refine vegetables, legumes or cereals.
If you want to eat vegetable soup immediately, add the desired vegetables half an hour before.
Refrigerate for later use.

9.7 Basic recipe for a fish soup

Strengthens kidney Qi and Yin, strengthens blood and fluids, promotes urination.
Cooking time approx. 40 min
Calories p. portion: 128
5 portions
Allergens: DLO

Quantity of ingredients
Fish pieces mixed (fresh water) 3/4 lbs / 300g. (recommended).water
Celery root 1/4 lbs - 4oz / 120g. (recommended) .... earth
Leek 2 inches / 10g. (recommended)..metal
Carrot 2 pieces / 150g. (yes) .... earth
White wine 1/2 cup / 125g. ()..wood
Lemon 1/2 piece / 50g. ()..wood
Bay leaf 2 leaves / 2g. (recommended) ....*
Peppercorns 3 pieces / 2g. ()..metal
Olive oil 1 table spoon / 10g. (yes)............................... earth
Water 2 cup / 450g. (yes) .... earth

Cooking instructions:
Fry celery, chopped carrots and leeks in olive oil, add bay leaf and peppercorns, add pieces of fish and sauté briefly. Add water, add little white wine or lemon. Simmer gently for 30 minutes. Skim off the resulting foam several times. In the end, sift the ingredients through a cloth. Refrigerate for later use.

9.8   Beluga lentil stew with vegetables

Tonifies Qi and blood, forces kidneys and spleen, dissipates heat and moisture.
Cooking time approx. 20 min
Calories p. portion: 201
5 portions

Quantity of ingredients

Lentils 1 1/2 cups / 240g. (recommended) ....water
Water 4-5 cups / 500g. (yes) .... earth
Carrot 3 pieces / 150g. (recommended)................................... earth
Leek 1 piece / 300g. (recommended) ....metal
Kohlrabi 1/2 piece / 200g. (recommended) .... earth
Tomato 2 pieces / 80g. (recommended) ....wood
Onion white 1 piece / 50g. (recommended)...............................metal
Bay leaf 2 leaves / 1g. (recommended) ....*
Fennel 1 piece / 250g. (recommended) .... earth
Star anise 2 pieces / 1g. (recommended) ....*
Juniper berry 6 pieces / 2g. (recommended)................................ fire
Olive oil 2 table spoons / 30g. (recommended) .... earth
Salt 1 pinch / 1g. (recommended)..water
Ginger fresh 1/2 teaspoon / 2g. (recommended)......................metal
Black caraway 1 pinch / 1g. (recommended) ....*

Cooking instructions:

Heat oil in hot pot. Fry onions and add diced vegetables and spices, lentils (washed well) and salt. Cover with cold water (3 fingers wide) and cook for 20 minutes on a low heat.
Sprinkle with fresh herbs and black cumin

Goes well with rice!

9.9   Cardamom water

Warms the middle, dissolves stagnation, directs upwards. Tonifies the kidney-Yang, nourishes bones and tendons, warms kidneys and spleen, forces stomach, dissolves flatulence, contracts, controls excessive urination, helps with digestive weakness.
Cooking time approx. 20 min
Calories p. portion: 16
4 portions

Quantity of ingredients
Cardamom 2 table spoons / 18g. (recommended) ....*
Water 4 cup / 1000g. (yes) .... earth

Cooking instructions:
Finely crush cardamom pods in a mortar. Boil with 1 liter of water and cook gently for 10 minutes over medium heat. Fill cardamom water through a sieve in glasses and serve hot.

9.10 Colorful tuscan bean soup

Cools heat, produces humors, nourishes Yin from heart and kidney, relaxes, builds up Qi, spreads.
Cooking time approx. 2 hours
Calories p. portion: 249
3 portions
Allergens: L

Quantity of ingredients
Kidney beans (red) 1/8 lbs - 2oz / 50g. (recommended)............water
Chickpeas 1 oz / 25g. (recommended) ....water
Lentils 1 oz / 25g. (recommended) ....water
Celery sticks 1 stick / 10g. (recommended)............................... earth
Tomato 2 pieces / 100g. (recommended) .... wood
Fennel seeds ground 1/2 teaspoon / 1g. (recommended) .... earth
Salt 1 pinch / 1g. (recommended)...water
Pepper (ground) 1 pinch / 0,5g. (recommended)........................metal
Garlic 1 clove / 3g. (recommended)...metal
Olive oil 2 table spoons / 50g. (recommended) .... earth
Water 2 1/4 cups / 500g. (yes)... earth
Basil (fresh) 5-7 leaves / 3g. (recommended) ....metal

Cooking instructions:
Soak legumes, boil and puree. Add vegetables, spices, herbs and oil and cook gently for 2 hours.

Variation: Sweet chestnuts give the dish a special Italian touch.

9.11 Cream cheese substitute

Cools heat, keeps fluids, builds up blood and Yin.
Cooking time approx. 20 min
Calories p. portion: 526
2 portions
Allergens: AE

Quantity of ingredients
Soybean milk 4 cup / 300g. (recommended)............................... earth
Lemon 1 piece / 50g. (recommended) ....wood
Herbs various 2 table spoons / 6g. (recommended)..........................*
Whole grain bread 6 slices / 300g. (recommended) ....wood

Cooking instructions:
Heat the soy milk in a saucepan till it boils, stirring occasionally (gets
burn easily!), Then allow to cool.
Squeeze out the lemon and stir gently under the cooled soy milk
(approx. 80°C/176°F), let it approx. 20 min. rest or clot.
Pour chopped soy milk through a strainer lined with a dishcloth, allow
liquid to drain and then squeeze out remaining liquid with the dishcloth.
Refine to taste with fresh herbs.
Serve with wholemeal bread.

9.12 Duck with mung beans

Nourishes Yin, reduces heat, softens, passes downwardly, forces
stomach und liver, regulates Qi flow, moisturizes, relaxes, spreads,
dissolves stagnation.
Cooking time approx. 2 hours
Calories p. portion: 747
5 portions
Allergens: E

Quantity of ingredients
Duck (slaughtered) 1/2 piece / 1250g. (recommended)..............wood
Onion white 2 pieces / 120g. (recommended)............................metal
Carrot 1 piece / 120g. (recommended) .... earth
Garlic 1 clove / 3g. (recommended)..metal
Mung bean 5/8 lbs - 8oz / 250g. (recommended)......................water
Peppercorns 3 pieces / 2g. (recommended) ....metal
Honey 1 teaspoon / 3g. (recommended)..................................... earth
Soy sauce 1 teaspoon / 3g. (recommended)..............................water
Lemon juice 1 teaspoon / 3g. (recommended)...........................wood

Salt 1 pinch / 1g. (recommended)..water
Pepper (ground) 1 pinch / 0,5g. (recommended).........................metal
Olive oil 1 table spoon / 10g. (recommended)........................... earth
Bay leaf 2 leaves / 2g. (recommended) ....*
Black caraway 1 pinch / 1g. (recommended) ....*
Savory 1 teaspoon / 2g. (recommended).................................water

Cooking instructions:
The day before soak the mung beans and rinse the duck cold. Wash
the vegetables, clean and cut into pieces. Put the duck and vegetables
in a saucepan and cover with water. Add bay leaves, savory, mugwort
and peppercorns. Boil over medium heat and simmer for 45 minutes.
Skim off the foam. Remove duck from the stock, allow to cool and keep
cool overnight.
In a saucepan, sauté the chopped onion in olive oil and pour in 1/4 liter
of stock and add the pre-cooked vegetables. Add the mung beans and
season with honey, soy sauce, lemon juice, salt, crushed black cumin
and pepper.
Serve with rice or potatoes.

9.13 Fish soup with rosemary

Strengthens kidney Qi, strengthens blood and fluids, promotes
urination, regulates Qi, dries out, passes downwardly, strengthens
spleen and liver, regulates Qi flow, moisturizes, relaxes, builds up Qi,
spreads.
Cooking time approx. 30 min
Calories p. portion: 271
4 portions
Allergens: DLO

Quantity of ingredients
Basic recipe for a fish soup 2 cup / 500g. (recommended)................*
Rosemary 1/2 bunch / 7g. (recommended).................................. fire
Onion (spring onion) 1 piece / 20g. (recommended) ....metal
Olive oil 2 table spoons / 35g. (recommended).......................... earth
Fish pieces mixed 5/8 lbs - 8oz / 250g. (recommended) ....water
Carrot 1 piece / 120g. (recommended) .... earth
Parsnip 1 piece / 180g. (recommended)...................................... fire
Celery root 1 slice / 20g. (recommended) .... earth
Salt 1 pinch / 1g. (recommended)..water
Peppercorns 2 pieces / 1g. (recommended) ....metal
Garlic 1 clove / 3g. (recommended)..metal

Cooking instructions:
Fry the onion and garlic in oil. Add fish broth. Add diced carrots, parsnips and celery. Season with salt and peppercorns. Simmer the soup on a low heat for 25 minutes.
Wash the fish, drizzle with lemon juice, divide into pieces and add to the soup with the pink rosemary. Cook for 5 min on low heat.
Add the chives and parsley and season the soup with the salt.

9.14 Fish soup with white wine, laurel and marjoram

Strengthens kidney Qi, strengthens blood and fluids, promotes urination, moisturizes, softens knots, regulates Qi, dries out, passes downwardly, relaxes, builds up Qi.
Cooking time approx. 45 min
Calories p. portion: 200
3 portions
Allergens: DLO

Quantity of ingredients
Onion (spring onion) 2 pieces / 40g. (recommended)................metal
Garlic 1 clove / 2g. (recommended)...metal
Basic recipe for a fish soup 2 cup / 500g. (recommended)................*
Carrot 1 piece / 60g. (recommended) .... earth
Parsnip 1 piece / 100g. (recommended) .... fire
Celery root 1 slice / 60g. (recommended) .... earth
Salt 1 pinch / 1g. (recommended)...water
Peppercorns 2 pieces / 1g. (recommended) ....metal
Lemon 1/4 piece / 10g. (recommended) .... wood
White wine 1/2 cup / 125g. (recommended).............................. wood
Bay leaf 2 leaves / 1g. (recommended) ....*
Rosemary 1 teaspoon / 2g. (recommended)................................ fire
Chives 1 teaspoon (chopped) / 3g. (recommended)..................metal
Parsley 1 teaspoon (chopped) / 3g. (recommended)................. wood

Cooking instructions:
Fry the onion and garlic in oil until translucent. Add fish broth. Add the diced carrot, parsnip and celery. Season with salt and peppercorns. Simmer the soup on a low heat for 25 minutes.
Wash the fish, drizzle with lemon juice, divide into pieces and add to the soup with the wine, the bay leaves and the marjoram. Cook for 5 min on low heat.
Add the chives and parsley and season the soup with the salt.

9.15 Fried asparagus with rocket

Nourishes Yin of lungs and kidney, feeds Yin, builds up Qi, forces Qi, strengthens spleen, guides damp heat down.
Cooking time approx. 15 min
Calories p. portion: 149
3 portions
Allergens: G

Quantity of ingredients
Butter organic 1 table spoon / 20g. (recommended).................. earth
Asparagus (green or white) 1,1 lbs / 500g. (recommended)....... earth
Pepper (ground) 1 pinch / 0,5g. (recommended)........................metal
Salt 1 pinch / 1g. (recommended)...water
Lemon 1/4 piece / 12g. (recommended) ....wood
Rucola 2 handful / 30g. (recommended)...................................... fire
Potato 3/4 lbs / 300g. (recommended)..................................... earth

Cooking instructions:
Melt a piece of butter in a hot pan; cut the peeled asparagus into pieces of 3 to 4 cm, fry for about 10 minutes until tender, but crisp. Sprinkle with freshly ground pepper, salt, add a few drops of lemon juice or finely grated lemon zest, finely shredded rucola leaves.
Cook the potatoes in plenty of salted water, then peel.

9.16 Hummus (Chickpeasmash)

Strengthens spleen and heart, softens, passes downwardly, moisturizes, relaxes, builds up Qi, spreads, nourishes blood, nourishes blood and liver, harmonizes liver and spleen, forces eyesight, preserves the fluids, contracts.
Cooking time approx. 2 hours
Calories p. portion: 542
2 portions
Allergens: N

Quantity of ingredients
Chickpeas 1 1/2 cups / 240g. (recommended)...........................water
Wakame 1 teaspoon (grated) / 2g. (recommended)..................water
Ginger fresh 1/4 teaspoon / 1g. (recommended)......................metal
Rosemary 1 pinch / 0,5g. (recommended)................................... fire
Sesame paste (Tahini) 1 table spoon / 10g. (recommended) ..... earth
Olive oil 2 table spoons / 20g. (recommended).......................... earth
Lemon juice 1 dach / 2g. (recommended)................................wood

Water upon need / g. (yes).. earth
Garlic 1 clove (scraped) / 2g. (recommended) ....metal
Parsley 1 teaspoon (chopped) / 2g. (recommended)................. wood
Peppers 1 pinch / 0,2g. (recommended)................................. earth
Curcuma 1 pinch / 0,2g. (recommended)......................................*
Coriander 1 pinch / 0,2g. (recommended)................................metal
Cardamom 1 pinch / 0,2g. (recommended)...................................*
Pepper (ground) 1 pinch / 0,2g. (recommended).......................metal
Salt (herbal) 1/2 teaspoon / 2g. (recommended).......................water

Cooking instructions:

Soak chickpeas overnight or for at least 6 hours, pour off soaking water, boil in fresh water for about 1 to 1 ½ hours with a little seaweed and ginger, allow to cool.
Seasoning with a few splashes of lemon juice and parsley.
Add the pepper, garlic cut into small pieces or pressed, more or less coriander and cardamom powder, little chilly powder as desired, tahin and olive oil. Puree all ingredients together. Depending on the consistency, add water. It should be a smooth paste.
Spread on cereal, crackers or toasted bread or enjoy with salad.

9.17 Indian Dal soup

Reduces internal heat and moisture, softens, passes downwardly, strengthens spleen and liver, regulates Qi flow, moisturizes, relaxes, builds up Qi, spreads, forces liver and kidney, reduces damp heat.
Cooking time approx. 30 min
Calories p. portion: 256
2 portions
Allergens: EN

Quantity of ingredients

Lentils 3/8 lbs - 6oz / 175g. (recommended) ....water
Sesame oil 2 table spoons / 30g. (recommended) .... earth
Carrot 1 piece / 100g. (recommended) .... earth
Onion (shallot) 1 piece / 15g. (recommended) ....metal
Water 1 1/2 cups / 200g. (yes)... earth
Ginger fresh 2 slices / 1g. (recommended) ....metal
Salt 1 pinch / 0,5g. (recommended)...water
Soy sauce 1 teaspoon / 3g. (recommended).............................water
Parsley 1 teaspoon (chopped) / 3g. (recommended)................. wood
Thyme 1 teaspoon / 3g. (recommended) ....*
Basil 1 table spoon / 5g. (recommended)...................................metal

Cooking instructions:
Soak the lentils overnight.
in a hot pot, carrot, onion and a little ginger fry, pour water. Add the lentils and cook until soft. Add salt or soy sauce and cook for another 10 minutes.
Stir in parsley before serving; Sprinkle thyme or basil over it.
Variant: Other herbs such as sage, rosemary or lovage allow a variety of flavors.

9.18 Legumes

Strengthens spleen and liver, regulates Qi flow, moisturizes, relaxes, builds up Qi, spreads, nourishes blood and Qi, diuretic, harmonizes Qi (in the middle and lower heater), detoxifies, reduces internal heat and moisture.
Cooking time approx. 30 min
Calories p. portion: 31
5 portions

Quantity of ingredients
Pinto beans speckled 1/4 lbs - 4oz / 100g. (recommended) .... water
Lentils 1/8 lbs - 2oz / 50g. (recommended) .... water
Peas, green 1/8 lbs - 2oz / 50g. (recommended) .... water
Water 4 cup / 1000g. (yes) .... earth
Lemon 1 slice / 2g. (recommended)... wood
Juniper berry 6 pieces / 2g. (recommended)................................ fire
Thyme 1 Twig / 3g. (recommended) ....*
Rosemary 1 Twig / 3g. (recommended)....................................... fire
Carrot 1 piece / 100g. (recommended) .... earth
Savory 1-2 teaspoons / 5g. (recommended) .... water
Ginger fresh a great piece / 3g. (recommended)........................ metal
Bay leaf 2-3 leaves / 1g. (recommended) ....*
Wakame 1-2 strips / 1g. (recommended) .... water

Cooking instructions:
Legumes such as beans, lentils, peas or chickpeas are soaked in plenty of cold water for several hours to three days. The water should be changed every 8 hours. Then pour off soaking water and wash legumes thoroughly.

Preparation:
Cook the legumes with fresh cold water and a slice of ginger and bring

to froth. Cook without lid for about 5 minutes, scooping off the foam. Only then add the following ingredients: a slice of lemon or lemon juice, crush juniper berries, thyme; (possibly 1 knife tip of asafoetida in case of severe indigestion). Add savory, sage, juniper, fenugreek seeds, carrots, bay leaves, fresh ginger, wakame algae.

Simmer on the slightest flame until beans or lentils have the desired consistency.
This base can be stored for 3-4 days in the refrigerator.

9.19 Radish with horseradish

Slightly refreshing and moisturizing, dissolves stagnation, nourishes blood and liver, harmonizes liver and spleen, forces eyesight, preserves the fluids, contracts, nourishes the lungs and spleen, distributes mucus, dissolves mucus, dissolves stagnation, directs upwards.
Cooking time approx. 30 min
Calories p. portion: 196
2 portions
Allergens: GNO

Quantity of ingredients
Butter organic 1 table spoon / 8g. (recommended) .... earth
Radish (white, green) 1/2 piece / 50g. (recommended) .... metal
Water 2 table spoons / 10g. (yes) .... earth
Lemon juice 2 table spoons / 20g. (recommended) .... wood
White wine 2 table spoons / 20g. (recommended) .... wood
Pepper powder (hot) 1 pinch / 0,2g. (recommended) .... fire
Sesame oil 1 teaspoon / 3g. (recommended) .... earth
Radish horseradish 2 table spoons / 20g. (recommended) .... metal
Salt 1 pinch / 0,5g. (recommended) .... water
Parsley 1 Bunch (chopped) / 80g. (recommended) .... wood
Rice long grain rice 1/2 cup / 60g. (recommended) .... metal
Water 3 cups / 300g. (yes) .... earth
Salt 1 pinch / 0,5g. (recommended) .... water

Cooking instructions:
In a hot pan melt the butter, sautéed into stripes cut radish. Add cold water, lemon juice, white wine, a pinch of rose paprika and stir in the sesame oil; with 2 - 3 tablespoons fresh grated horseradish (alternatively 1 teaspoon from the glass), salt to taste; Sprinkle with chopped parsley.
Place the rice with the water, salt and cook for about 15 minutes.

9.20 Refreshing cucumber soup with potatoes

Reduces damp heat, detoxifies, forces Qi, forces spleen, relieves inflammation, spreads.
Cooking time approx. 15 min
Calories p. portion: 148
3 portions
Allergens: GN

Quantity of ingredients
Sesame oil 1 table spoon / 10g. (recommended)........................ earth
Potato 4 pieces / 300g. (recommended) .... earth
Onion (spring onion) 3 pieces / 60g. (recommended)................ metal
Pepper (ground) 1 pinch / 0,5g. (recommended)........................ metal
Nutmeg 1 pinch / 1g. (recommended).. metal
Salt 1 pinch / 1g. (recommended).. water
Lemon 1/2 piece / 25g. (recommended) .... wood
Cucumber 2 pieces / 500g. (recommended) .... earth
Cream, sweet 30% 1 table spoon / 10g. (recommended).................. *
Dill 1 table spoon / 15g. (recommended) .... metal

Cooking instructions:
Sauté sesame oil, chopped potatoes, plenty of spring onions in a hot pot; add pepper, a little nutmeg, salt, lemon juice, hot water, diced cucumber; simmer for about 10 minutes and then puree; add some sweet cream as you like, fresh dill.

Variation: Add a little chili, oregano, thyme or rosemary to soften the cooling effect.

9.21 Rhubarb and apple jelly

Moisturizes, relaxes, builds up Qi, spreads, cools heat, preserves the fluids, contracts, strengthens middle heater, moisturizes, cools heat, distributes mucus, derives wind-cold and wind-heat, brings the stomach Qi in motion, solves congestion.
Cooking time approx. 15 min
Calories p. portion: 180
2 portions

Quantity of ingredients
Rhubarb 5/8 oz / 200g. (recommended) .... wood
Apple juice (natural cloudy) 1 cup / 300g. (recommended)......... earth
Corn starch 1 oz / 30g. (recommended).................................... earth

Honey 1/2 oz / 20g. (recommended)... earth
Vanilla sugar natural 1 pinch / 0,5g. (recommended) ....*
Cinnamon ground 1 pinch / 0,5g. (recommended) ....*
Peppermint 2 leaves / 2g. (recommended) ....metal

Cooking instructions:
Add the cornstarch to a 1/2 cup apple juice.
Simmer the rhubarb in 1 cup of water for 10 min.
Add the remaining apple juice and the cornstarch, stir, heat till it boils again.
Sweet with honey and season with vanilla and cinnamon. Spread the mixture on dessert bowls and garnish with mint.

9.22 Spring salad

Preserves the fluids, nourishes liver-Yin, cools heat, produces humors, moves Qi and blood, diuretic, cools in internal heat, dissolves stagnation, passes downwardly.
Cooking time approx. 10 min
Calories p. portion: 162
4 portions
Allergens: AEMN

Quantity of ingredients
Sorrel 3/8 lbs - 6oz / 150g. (recommended)...............................wood
Dandelion (young plants) 1/4 lbs - 4oz / 100g. (recommended)..... fire
Mung bean sprouting 0,2 lbs / 75g. (recommended) ....water
Cress 1/4 lbs - 4oz / 100g. (recommended) ....metal
Chives 1 Bunch / 50g. (recommended).....................................metal
Tomato 2 pieces / 100g. (recommended) ....wood
Parsley 1 Bunch / 50g. (recommended)....................................wood
Sesame paste (Tahini) 2 table spoons / 16g. (recommended) ... earth
Soy sauce 1 dash / 3g. (recommended) ....water
Mustard 1/2 teaspoon / 2g. (recommended) ....metal
White bread (wheat bread) 6 slices / 120g. (recommended) ......wood

Cooking instructions:
Wash all salad´s, mix and prepare the sauce as follows:
Mix tahini with mustard and balsamic vinegar, tamari, olive oil, chives and half of parsley. Pour the sauce over the salad and sprinkle the remaining parsley just before serving.
Serve with the white bread.

9.23 Tea from lavender blossoms

Cooking time approx. 10 min
Calories p. portion: 0
1 portions

Quantity of ingredients
Lavender blossoms 1 teaspoon / 2g. (recommended)......................*
Water 1 cup / 125g. (yes) .... earth

Cooking instructions:
Heat the water till it boils and put it aside. Add lavender flowers and 10 min. to let go. Sweet to taste with honey. Strain when pouring.

9.24 Tea from raspberry leaves

Strengthens spleen Qi.
Cooking time approx. 10 min
Calories p. portion: 0
1 portions

Quantity of ingredients
Raspberry leaf tea 2 table spoons / 4g. (recommended) ....*
Water 1 cup / 250g. (yes) .... earth

Cooking instructions:
Heat the water till it boils and put it aside. Add raspberry leaves and leave for 10 min. to let go. Sweet to taste with honey. Strain when pouring.

10 Effects of food

10.1 Use ingredients: recommendable

Acai powder
Acerola fruit nectar or powder
Adzuki beans
Agar agar (kelp)
Agave nectar
Agrimony
Almond
Almond marzipan
Almond milk
Almond puree
Aloe juice
Amaranth
Amaranth Pops
Anchovy / Sardine
Angelica root
Anise (Common Fennel)
Apple (sour)
Apple (sweet)
Apple juice (natural cloudy)
Apple puree
Apricot
Apricot dried
Apricot jam
Apricot nectar
Apricots
Apricots juice
Arrowroot
Artichoke
Asparagus (green or white)
Aubergine
Avocado
Baking powder
Balm
Bamboo shoots
Banana
Banana (cooking banana)
Banchatee (green tea)
barberry
Barley
Barley flour
Barley grass powder
Barley grouts
Barley malt
Barley not peeled
Basic recipe for a beef soup
Basic recipe for a beef soup (warming)
Basic recipe for a chicken soup (warming)
Basic recipe for a duck soup
Basic recipe for a fish soup
Basic recipe for a rice soup (Congee)
Basic recipe for a vegetable soup (nutritious)
Basil
Basil (fresh)
Batavia
Bay leaf
Bean oil
Beans (green, fresh)
Bearberry leaf
Beef bone marrow
Beef fillet
Beef heart
Beef heart (calf)
Beef kidney
Beef liver
Beef lungs (calf)
Beef meat
Beef meat (calf)
Beef meatbones
Beef Oxtail pieces
Beef soup meat
Beef stomach
Beer (alcohol-free)
Beer (alcohol-reduced)
Beer (Pils)
Beer (Top-fermented German dark beer)
Berries of the season
Berry juice
Bitter Herb liqueur
Bitter Lemon
Bitter liqueur
Bitter orange peel
Black beans
Black caraway
Black fungus mushroom
Black tea
Blackberry dried (unripe fruit)
Blackberry jam
Blackberry leaves
Blackberry´s
Black-eyed peas
Blackthorn (Sloe)
Blue mallow tee
Blueberry
Blueberry dried
Blueberry jam

Blueberry juice
Bocksdorn fruits (Fructus Lycii, Goji,
goji berry dried
Boletus mushroom
Borage
Borage oil
Boxhorn clover seeds
Brazil nuts
Bread roll
Bread with carob kernel flour
Breadcrumbs (wheat bread, bread roll)
Brie cheese
Broad beans (thick beans)
Broccoli
Brown ale
Brussels sprouts
Buckbean
Buckwheat
Buckwheat (roasted) Kasha
Buckwheat whole grain
Bulgur (cereals)
Burdock root tea
Bush beans
Butter (half fat)
Butter beans white
Butter organic
Buttermilk
Calamari
Camembert
Campari
Cantaloupe
Capers in olive oil
Carambola (Star fruit)
Cardamom
Carob flour, St. john's bread
Carp
Carrot
Carrot (Early Carrot)
Carrot juice without sugar
Cashews
Cauliflower
Caviar
Celery root
Celery sticks
Cereal coffee
Chamomile
Chamomile tea
Champignon
Channa-Dal
Chanterelle
Chard
Chenpi (chinese tangerine bowl)
Cherry
Cherry (sour)

Cherry compote
Cherry juice
Chervil
Chervil dried
Chestnut puree
Chestnuts
Chicken Blood
Chicken egg
Chicken egg white
Chicken heart
Chicken liver
Chicken meat
Chicken stomach
Chicken yolk
Chickpeas
Chickweed
Chicory
Chili (pod or ground)
Chinese cabbage
Chinese pearl barley
Chives
Chlorella (fresh water)
Chocolate
Chocolate (Diabetic)
Chrysanthemum blossom tea
Cinnamon ground
Cinnamon sticks
Clarified butter
Clementine
Clementines
Clove
Cocoa
Coconut fat
Coconut flakes
Coconut grated
Coconut meat
Coconut milk
Cod
Codfish
Coffee
Coix (seeds) YiYi Ren
Cola drink
Cola drink (low calorie)
Compote (fruits of the season)
Cooking oil
Coriander
Coriander (fresh)
Corn
Corn (fast polenta)
Corn (roasted)
Corn flour
Corn germ oil
Corn Grease (Polenta)
Corn silk tea

Corn starch
Cottage cheese
Couscous
Cow's milk (1.5% fat)
Cow's milk (whole milk 3.5% fat)
Crab
Cranberries
Cranberry
Cranberry
Cranberry jam
Cranberry juice
Cream (30% fat)
Cream 10% coffee cream
Cream sour 10%
Cream sour 20%
Cream sour 30%
Cream, sweet 30%
Creamer
Créme fraiche cheese
Cress
Crispbread
Crucian
Cucumber
Cucumber (bitter)
Cucumber (spicy cucumber)
Cumin (Caraway seed)
Curcuma
Curd cheese 20%
Curd cheese 40%
Currant (black)
Currant (red)
Currant (white)
Currant jam (black)
Currant jam (red)
Currant juice (black)
Currants (black)
Currants (red)
Curry
Curry paste red
Daisy
Dandelion (young plants)
Dandelion juice
Dandelionroots tea
Dashi
Dates dried
Dates red
Deer meat
Deer meat
Deer's Bones
Deer's kidneys
Dill
Duck (heart)
Duck (slaughtered)
Ducks egg

Dulse (seaweed)
Dyer's broom herb
Edam cheese
Eel
Eel smoked
Elderberries
Elderberry blossom tee
Emmental cheese
Endive salad
Evening primrose oil
Fennel
Fennel seeds ground
Fennel tea
Fenugreek (Trigonella foenum-
graecum)
Fernet Branca (herbal bitter liqueur)
Feta cheese
Feta cheese
Fig
Fig dried
Fish innards
Fish pieces mixed (fresh water)
Fish remains
Fish sauce
Flounder
Flower pollen
Fox nut, gorgon nut, makhana
French beans
Fresh cheese
Fresh cheese from soya
Fresh cheese with herbs
Freshwater crab
Freshwater fish
Fructose (glucose)
Fruit mix juice
Fruit tea
Gail plum
Galangal
Garam Masala powder
Garlic
Gelatin white
Gelee Royal
Gentian root
Gentian root tea
Ginger fresh
Ginger oil
Ginger powder
Ginkgo fruit
Ginseng
Ginseng liqueur
Ginseng root
Goat
Goat and sheep's blood
Goat and sheep's brain

Goat and sheep's liver
Goat and sheep's milk
Goat and sheep's stomach
Goat cheese
Goose
Goose blood
Goose egg
Goose fat
Goose parts
Gooseberry
Gorgonzola
Gouda cheese
Gourd
Grape juice red
Grape juice white
Grapefruit (Pomelo)
Grapefruit dried peel
Grapefruit juice
Grapes red
Grapes white
Grapeseed oil
Grass carp
Green spelt
Green tea
Greengage
Ground
Ground caraway
Guava
Halibut (Flatfish)
Hawthorn
Hazelnuts
Herbal tea mix
Herbs bitter
Herbs of Provence
Herbs various
Herbs wild
Herring
Hibiscus
Hibiscus tea
Hijiki
Hokkaido pumpkin
Honey
Honey wine (Met)
Hop
Horehound leaves
Horse meat
Hyssop
Iceberg lettuce
Jasmine blossoms tee
Jellyfish
Juniper berry
Kaki plum
Kalmus
Kefir

Kidney beans (red)
King Solomon's-seal
Kiwi
Kohlrabi
Kombu seaweed (Saccharina japonica)
Kudzu
Kukicha tea
Kumquats
Ladyfingers
Lamb bones
Lamb kidneys
Lamb liver
Lamb meat
Lamb shoulder
Lamb's lettuce
Lamb's lettuce
Lavender blossoms
Leaf salads (bitter)
Leek
Lemon
Lemon Balm (dried)
Lemon Balm (fresh)
Lemon juice
Lemon peel
Lemongrass
Lentils
Lentils black
Lentils red
Lentils yellow
Lettuce
Licorice root tea
Lily bulbs
Lima beans
Lime
Lime blossom tea
Linseed
Linseed (crushed)
Linseed oil
Liver smoothing tea
Lobster
Longane
Loquate / Japanese medlar
Lotus roots
Lotus seeds
Lovage
Lovage seeds
Luo Han Guo fruit
Lychee
Lychee in Preserved
Lychee liqueur
Lye roll
Mackerel
Mallow (Malva sylvestris) blossom tea
Malt

Mango
Mango juice
Manioc flour
Maple syrup
Mare's milk
Margarine
Margarine (diet)
Marjoram
Martini
Mascarpone cheese
Mayonnaise 50%
Mayonnaise 80%
Mediterranean fish (cod, plaice, haddock, sea eel, mackerel)
Medlar
Millet
Millet flakes
Mineral water
Mirabelle plum
Miso
Miso black (fermented)
Miso paste (soy bean paste)
Mixed Pickles
Mold cheese
Morel (black, dried)
Morel, dried
Mozzarella
Mu Erh Mushroom
Muesli
Mulberry fruit
Mulled Wine Spice
Mullet
Multi-grain bread (gray bread)
Mung bean
Mung bean sprouting
Mussels
Mustard
Mustard Dijon
Mustard medium hot
Mustard seeds
Mustard sweet
Mutton
Mutton
Nasturtium (nose-twister or nose-tweaker)
Nectarine
Nettles
Noodles (wheat) with egg
Noodles (wheat, lasagne) with egg
Noodles (wheat, ribbon noodles) with egg
Noodles (wheat, spaghetti) with egg
Noodles (whole grain) with egg
Nori, purple seaweed, red algae

Nutmeg
Oat
Oat flakes (whole grain)
Oat flakes roasted
Oat flour
Oat fusion (baby food)
Oat meal
Oat milk
Octopus
Octopus
Okra
Olive oil
Olives
Olives green
Onion (shallot)
Onion (spring onion)
Onion read
Onion white
Orange
Orange blossom
Orange dried peel
Orange grated peel
Orange jam
Orange juice
Orange peel
Oregano dried
Oregano fresh
Oyster mushroom
Oyster shell powder
Oysters
Palm oil
Papaya
Parmesan
Parsley
Parsley root
Parsnip
Passion blossoms tea
Passion fruit
Peaches
Peaches (canned)
Peanut (roasted)
Peanut butter
Peanut oil
Peanuts
Pear
Pear juice
Pearl barley
Pearl barley
Peas
Peas, green
Pepper (ground)
Pepper Cayenne
Pepper powder (hot)
Pepper white (ground)

Peppercorns
Peppermint
Peppermint tea
Pepperoni
Pepperoni, red, pitted, halved
Pepperoni, yellow, pitted, halved
Peppers
Peppers (rose peppers)
Peppers (sweet)
Peppers powder
Perch
Pheasant
Pickle
Pig blood
Pigeon
Pigeon egg
Pimento
Pine nuts
Pineapple
Pineapple (from a can)
Pineapple juice without sugar
Pinto beans speckled
Pistachios
Plaice
Plum
Plum dried
Plums
Pomegranate
Poppy
Pork Bacon
Pork brain
Pork fat (lard)
Pork ham
Pork ham cooked
Pork ham smoked
Pork heart
Pork kidneys
Pork knuckle
Pork Lard
Pork liver
Pork lung
Pork marrow bones
Pork meat
Pork sausage (Bratwurst)
Pork skin
Pork stomach
Pork/beef sausage (smoked)
Pork's intestine
Potato
Potato (mealy)
Potato flour
Prickly pear
Processed cheese 12%
processed cheese 30%

Prosecco
Psyllium seed
Pudding powder vanilla
Puff pastry
Pumpernickel (dark bread)
Pumpkin
Pumpkin seed oil
Pumpkin seeds
Quail
Quail egg
Quince
Quinoa
Rabbit
Rabbit (wild)
Rabbit liver
Rabbit meat
Radicchio
Radish
Radish (white, green, purple-red)
Radish black
Radish horseradish
Radish leaves
Raisins
Rapeseed oil
Raspberry
Raspberry dried (immature)
Raspberry jam
Raspberry leaf tea
Red beet
Red berry (without sugar)
Red cabbage
Red wine
Reishi mushroom
Rhubarb
Ribworttea
Rice (fragrance)
Rice (Gaoliang / Sorghum)
Rice (whole grain)
Rice Basmati
Rice black
Rice flour
Rice long grain rice
Rice malt
Rice mash
Rice noodles
Rice red
Rice round grain
Rice starch
Rice sticky
Rice sweet
Rice variety any
Rice wild (nature rice)
Romaine lettuce / lettuce salad
Rose blossom tea

Rose hip
Rose hip tea
Rose leaf tea
Rosefish
Rosemary
Rucola
Rum
Rusk
Rye
Rye flour
Rye wholemeal bread
Safflower (Dyer's thistle / Hong Hua)
Saffron
Sage
Sago (cereals)
Sake
Salmon
Salsify
Salt
Salt (herbal)
Sauerkraut (cutted cabbage fermented)
Savory
Savoy cabbage / kale
Sea buckthorn
Sea cucumber
Seacrab
Sesame oil
Sesame oil roasted
Sesame paste (Tahini)
Sesame, black
Sesame, white
Shark
Sheep's milk
Sheep's milk yoghurt
Sherry (whine)
Shiitake, dried
Shrimp
Shrimps
Skim milk powder
Slug
Sorrel
Sour cherries
Sour cream 15% fat
Sour milk
Sour milk cheese 20%
Sourdough
Soy flour
Soy noodles
Soy sauce
Soy Tofu
Soy Tofu smoked
Soya Cuisine (soy cream)
Soybean milk
Soybean oil

Soybeans
Soybeans, black
Soybeans, blacks, fermented
Soybeans, yellow
Spelled flakes
Spinach
Spiny lobsters
Spirit
Spurdog (spiny dogfish, Schillerlocken)
St. Benedict's thistle, blessed thistle,
holy thistle, spotted thistle
Star anise
Stevia (candyleaf, sweetleaf)
Strawberries
Strawberry jam
Strawberry Juice
Sugar - icing sugar
Sugar brown
Sugar candy white
Sugar cane sugar
Sugar fructose - fruit sugar
Sugar glucose - grapes sugar
Sugar Milk Sugar
Sugar molasses
Sugar palm sugar
Sugar substitute (sweetener)
Sugar white
Sunflower oil
Sunflower seeds
Supplementary nutrition
Sweet potato
Tabasco
Tangerine
Tarragon (Estragon)
Tea mixture uric acid lowering
Thistle oil
Thyme
Thyme dried
Toast bread (whole grain)
Tomato
Tomato dried
Tomato juice
Tomato paste
Tomato puree
Tonic Water
Topinambur
Trout
Trout (smoked)
Truffle
Tsampa (roasted barley flour)
Tuna
Turkey breast meat
Turkey ham
Turmeric (yellow root)

Turnip
Turnips
Umeboshi paste
Umeboshi plums (Japanese apricots)
Valerian
Vanilla
Vanilla pod
Vanilla powder
Vanilla sugar natural
Vegetable juice
Vinegar (Apple vinegar)
Vinegar (Red wine vinegar)
Vinegar Aceto Balsamico
Vinegar Aceto Balsamico white
Wakame
Walnut oil
Walnuts
Walnuts roasted
Watermelon
Wax gourd
Wheat
Wheat beer
Wheat bran
Wheat bulgur
Wheat flakes
Wheat flatbread/pita bread
Wheat flour
Wheat flour whole grain
Wheat germ oil
Wheat semolina
Wheat semolina for children
Wheat/Rye/Gray-black bread with yeast

Wheatgrass juice
Wheatgrass powder
Whey
White beans
White bread (baguette)
White bread (pretzel sticks)
White bread (roll)
White bread (wheat bread)
White breadcrumbs
White cabbage
White dumpling bread (wheat bread cut into chunks)
White wine
Whitefish
Whole grain bread
Wholemeal flour
Wild boar meat
Wild garlic (garlic spinach)
Wild herbs
Wild strawberries
Wormwood
Wormwood herb
Yam root, yam root tuber
Yarrow
Yarrow tea
Yeast
Yew nut
Yoghurt vanilla
Yogi tea
Yogurt (natural, 1.5% fat)
Yogurt (natural, 3.5% fat)
Zucchini

10.2 Use ingredients: yes

Water

Water hot

10.3 Do not use contra-acting foods

Spelled (Dark) bread

Spelled grain

11 Herbs and their effects

11.1 Basil

thermal effect: warm
taste: spicy, bitter
Dries out, leads down. Tonifies Yang and Qi, dissolves mucus-cold, eliminates wind-cold.
It has a beneficial effect on flatulence and nausea, relaxing and soothing.

Good to fight emphysema, bronchitis, whooping cough, high blood pressure, headache, mouth odor, warts, hiccup, gout, migraine.

11.2 Mugwort

thermal effect: warm
taste: bitter, spicy
Regulates and nourishes bleeding, warms the inside, eliminates wind-cold, eliminates parasites, eliminates heat, wetness, regulates and moves Qi.
Reduces bleeding, alleviates pain. In the kitchen, mugwort is used as a spice for fat food. Since it contains many bitter substances, it boosts fat burning and promotes digestion.

11.3 Savory

thermal effect: warm
taste: bitter
Tonifies kidney yang, heart qi, stomach and spleen qi and warms the middle, moves the liver qi and blood, releases mucous and cold from the lungs, opens the surface, induces wind-cold.
Stomach-strengthening, soothing and appetizing. Ideal for prevent colds, strengthens the immune system. In case of incontinence or nocturnal wetting (not for children), put the beans in liquor for libido.

11.4 Dill

thermal effect: warm
taste: spicy
Moves qi, triggers stagnation, heads up.
The medicinal and spice herb has an antispasmodic effect and stimulates gastric juice production. Good to fight flatulence. Antispasmodic for gastrointestinal discomfort.

11.5 Coriander

thermal effect: warm
taste: spicy
Driving sweat, reducing wind, draining moisture, tonifying and regulating qi, eliminating wind-cold.
The essential oils are appetizing, digestive, cramping and soothing in stomach and intestinal disorders.

11.6 Herbs various

Stimulates appetite. Effect different.
Appetizing, lots of trace elements and vitamins.

11.7 Cress

thermal effect: cool
taste: sweet
Moves and tonifies qi and blood, diuretic, cools in internal heat,
moisturizes lungs, triggers stagnation, heads upwards.
Diuretic, supports urination. Good to fight dry mouth, inner agitation, sore
throat, diabetes, kidney stones, gastrointestinal complaints, lung
problems, menstrual cramps or cancer.

11.8 Chives

thermal effect: warm
taste: spicy
Directs upward. Tonifies blood, kidney Yang and Qi. Dissolves moisture.
Bactericide, prevents cancer, strengthens gastric juice production,
promotes digestion and blood circulation, promotes growth, triggers
stagnation.

11.9 Lavender blossoms

thermal effect: warm
taste: spicy, bitter
Do not use during pregnancy. Suppresses internal wind, dissipates
moisture and heat. Regulates and moves Qi, tones Qi, moves blood,
eliminates heat, reduces fire.
Calms the central nervous system, relieves anxiety, to fight sleep
disturbances, loss of appetite and nervous intestinal complaints.

11.10   Lily bulbs

thermal effect: cool
taste: sweet, bitter
Tonifies Yin, soothes Shen / Spirit. Moisturizes the lungs, clears heat and
stops coughing.
Calms nerves, good to fight scaly skin. The onions and the petals are
added to ointments in the Orient, which can heal muscles and tendons.
White lily (astringent).

11.11   Dandelion (young plants)

thermal effect: cool
taste: sweet, bitter
Cools liver-heat, reduces internal heat, softens knots, eliminates heat, reduces fire, dissolves mucus heat, moves blood, tonifies qi.
Detoxifies, relieves inflammation. Regulates digestion, helps with rheumatism, releases kidney stones, leaves pimples and chronic skin disorders disappear.

11.12   Parsley

thermal effect: warm
taste: bitter
Nourishes blood and liver, harmonizes liver and spleen, strengthens eyesight, preserves juices, contracts. Dissolves moisture and warms Yang.
Stimulates liver function, detoxifies. Forces urinating. Relieves flatulence. Digestive and menstrual stimulating, birth-accelerating, memory-enhancing, blood-purifying, skin-smoothing.

11.13   Peppermint

thermal effect: cool
taste: spicy, bitter
Cools heat, expels mucus, dissipates wind-cold and wind-heat, moves stomach qi, releases congestion, tonifies, regulates and moves qi.
Relaxes, frees the lungs and the nose (inhale), regulates the cycle.
Stimulates bile flow and bile production, antispasmodic in gastrointestinal disorders, antimicrobial and antiviral.

11.14   Rosemary

thermal effect: warm
taste: bitter
Dries out, leads down. Strengthens the heart, lungs and spleen qi, strengthens liver blood. Strengthens heart-Yin. Expels spleen heat / cold moisture. Strengthens spleen and kidney yang.
Promotes digestion, relieves bloating, strengthens lung, spleen and kidney. Affects the circulation and nerves. Appetizing. Baths help to fight circulatory disorders as well as with gout and rheumatism.

11.15 Sorrel

thermal effect: cold
taste: sour
Protects the fluids, pull together.
Astringent, hematopoietic, purifies the blood, diuretic. Good to fight liver weakness, upset stomach, indigestion, constipation, diarrhea, worms, scurvy, anemia, women's complaints, wounds, skin rashes, boils, ulcers, swelling.

11.16 Black caraway

thermal effect: warm
taste: spicy, sweet
Dissolve / transform moisture, tonifyes Yang and Qi, moves blood, suppresses inner wind.
Detoxifying, immunoregulatory. In addition, the oil should stimulate the formation of bone marrow cells and generally protect body cells from viruses.

11.17 King Solomon's-seal

thermal effect: neutral
taste: sweet, bitter
Tonifies Yin and Qi, astringent, tonifies blood, eliminates wind-cold / heat-wetness.
Used to repair wounds or damaged tissue. Good to fight dry cough, earlier also tuberculosis and dysentery, as well as diarrhea and hemorrhoids.

11.18 Yam root, yam root tuber

thermal effect: neutral
taste: sweet
Tonifies Yin, Yang and Qi, reduces inner wind, dissolves wetness, warms Yang.
Solves cramps (in the gastrointestinal tract). Digestive through increased bile production. Anti-inflammatory in rheumatic diseases.
Mucolytic agent for coughing. Relief of menopausal symptoms.

12 Basics of Nutrition

The basic principles of nutrition described herein are general recommendations. They are not aimed at a specific form of therapy. Recommendations concerning a therapy have priority.

12.1 Nutrition

Regular meals in a relaxed atmosphere. A warm breakfast is considered a good start into the day.

The main meals ought to be taken for lunch – supper in the early evening. Pay attention to feeling hungry or sated: don't eat too much nor remain hungry is the rule

Prepare the meals freshly from natural, regional products. Frozen, heat-conserved, industrially prepared or foodstuffs cooked in the microwave oven are rejected.

Choice of foodstuffs according to the season: more cooling food in summer, more warming food in winter.

Eat cooked food at least twice a day. Food and drinks ought to be lukewarm, never ice-cold or hot.

Raw vegetables, briefly cooked vegetables, freshly squeezed juices and mineral water are not recommended. Milk and dairy products are only included in the diet if they don't cause problems. Don't use therapeutic recipes over a longer period without consulting your doctor or therapist.

Varied food
Enjoy the diversity of foodstuffs. Characteristics of a balanced nutrition are variety, suitable combination and a balanced quantity of rich and low energy foodstuffs (on one hand avoiding undersupply with essential nutrients and on the other hand to take to many undesirable substances).

A lot of Cereal Products - and Potatoes
Bread, pasta, rice, cereal flakes (best wholemeal) as well as potatoes contain almost no fat, but many vitamins, mineral nutrients, trace elements, roughage and secondary plant substances. These foodstuffs ought to be taken with low-fat side dishes.

Vegetables and Fruit – „Take Five" every day ... 5 portions of
vegetables and fruit a day, as fresh as possible, briefly cooked, or maybe one portion as a juice – ideal as a side dish to every meal as well as snack between meals: Thus a lot of vitamins, mineral nutrients as well as roughage and secondary plant substances

Daily milk and dairy products
Milk and Dairy Products every Day, once or twice per Week Fish; meat, sausages as well as eggs moderately. These foodstuffs contain valuable nutrients like calcium in the milk, iodine selenium and omega-3 fat acids in saltwater fish. Meat is favorable due to its high content of disposable iron and the vitamins B1, B6 and B12. Quantities of 300 – 600 g meat and sausage per week are sufficient. Prefer low-fat products, especially in meat- and dairy products.

Low-fat and fatty Foodstuffs
Fat supplies us with essential fat acids and fatty foodstuffs contain also fat-soluble vitamins. Fat is high in energy; therefore much fat in the food may cause overweight, possibly also cancer. Too many saturated fat acids may further a tendency for cardio-vascular diseases in the long term. Prefer vegetable oils and fats (e.g. rapeseed-, olive-, soya-oils and solid fats produced therefrom). Beware of invisible fat in meat- and dairy products, pastry and sweets as well as in fast-food and convenience foods. 70 – 90 g fat per day is sufficient.

Moderately Sugar and Salt
Take sugar and foods/drinks containing various kinds of sugar (e.g. glucose syrup) only occasionally. Use herbs and spices as well as a little salt creatively. Prefer salt containing iodine.

Plenty of Liquids
Water is absolutely essential. Drink 1-2 l liquids every day. Prefer water (with or without gas) and other low-calorie drinks. Alcoholic drinks should not be taken.

Tasty Dishes, carefully cooked
Cook the meals with as low temperatures and as short as possible, using little water and fat – this preserves the original taste, keeps the nutrients intact and prevents the production of harmful compounds.

Take time and enjoy the food
Take your Time and enjoy your Food
Eating consciously helps to eat right. The eye enjoys food, too. It's fun, invites to enjoy varied dishes and stimulates the feeling of satiety.

Watch your Weight and stay in Motion
A balanced diet and a lot of exercise and sport (30 – 60 min/day) are a healthy combination. The right weight furthers well-being and health. Thermals, directional effectiveness, digestive power

There are various criteria for judging the effectiveness of herbs and foodstuffs.

The use of certain herbs and ingredients is based on observations of the effects on the body which these foodstuffs, herbs and spices show after having eaten them. The medical science has developed following system: Every ingredient or herb has a directional effectiveness. Furthermore, there are herbs which have a special effect on certain organs.

The basic condition for a healthy metabolism is to obtain sufficient energy from food and that the digestive process doesn't use too much energy. An easily digestible meal makes content and sated, doesn't cause flatulence and fatigue after the meal. The perfect spices increase the healthiness of our meals. Very often, just small doses of herbs and spices will suffice. They are not used to make us sated, but to help our digestive organs to digest the food.

12.2 Recipes

The recipes list the ingredients to be used and the cooking instructions show how the dish is prepared. The list of ingredients shows the concerned quantities as well as the relevance for the therapy. If you find „less than mentioned", try to comply or find an alternative from the „list of recommended foodstuffs". Mostly it shall result just in a small change of taste when you simply avoid this ingredient.

Mild cooking methods: boiling, stewing, poaching, steaming
Strong cooking methods: barbecuing, roasting, frying, smoking
Balanced cooking methods: deep-frying, baking brick
Deep-freezing and warming in the microwave oven should be avoided (denaturalization).

12.3 Foodstuffs

Foodstuffs have an effect on body and soul like medicinal herbs, only a very much milder one. Dietary advice is mainly based on regional foodstuffs. The knowledge about the effects of each foodstuff and the knowledge, when which foodstuff shall be used, is based on the orthodox school of medicine. Use ecologic-organic products, if possible. As everything should be cooked for a long time due to a better digestability and very rarely eaten raw, the food agrees with everyone.

The classification of the foodstuffs according to their effect on the body is the basis in order to achieve a harmonious status of health.

Dietary advisors do not recommend certain foodstuffs for everyone. The individual diet is tailor-made for the individual constitution.

Buy only fresh and ripe fruit and vegetables. You ought to leave unripe fruit and vegetables and such with brown spots and wilted leaves behind in the market. In this case take deep-frozen goods (never ready-to-serve dishes!). Fruit and vegetables are deep-frozen immediately after harvesting and often contain more vitamins and minerals than the goods from the vegetable shelf. Whereas conserved or tinned goods contain very much less biological substances. Also, salt, sugar and others are mostly added to the latter. Never leave the foodstuffs in the water after washing them to avoid that many vital substances get drowned. Clean salads, fruit and vegetables immediately before serving.

Please make sure of the hygienic processing of foodstuffs. Clean your salads, fruit and vegetables carefully. When cooking with meat, prepare all ingredients first and then process the meat products. Clean the worktop and tools very carefully. Wooden surfaces ought to be treated with a mild disinfectant regularly in order to reduce germination. Store fruit and vegetables separately, if possible. Harvested fruit and vegetables are still alive and emit e.g. ethylene gas, which makes other products ripen and age faster. Keep meat and fish in the closed packaging or store them in the fridge in closed containers.

12.4 Herbs

There are some basic rules for storing medicinal herbs. On principle, herbs must be protected from direct sunlight, humidity and heat.

Containers for the storage of herbs may be glasses, ceramic jars and even plastic containers. However, plastic is a rather unsuitable material and should only be a short-term solution. In case of glass containers, use a dark material.

Medicinal herbs cannot be kept for any long period. The shelf life of herbs is limited. However, it can be prolonged with suitable storage. The place should be dark, rather cool and absolutely dry. A wooden medicine cabinet, placed not directly next to a source of heat, would be ideal. Never buy large quantities of herbs so as not to have to throw them away. Label the container with the name of the herb and the date of harvesting or processing.

13 Other dietic-books

The following syndromes of dietetics, TCM or for a therapy supplement for cancer are available.

Dietetics
E001. Nutrition of the infant - baby food
E002. Nutrition during lactation
E003. Nutrition in old age
E004. Nutrition of children and adolescents
E005. Nutrition of athletes
E006. Light weight
E007. Pregnancy
E008. Full food

Protein and electrolyte - kidneys
E009. (hemodialysis) dialysis treatment
E010. Acute renal failure
E011. Chronic renal insufficiency
E012. Nephrotic syndrome
E013. Kidney stones (nephrolithiasis)

Gastrointestinal tract - pancreas
E014. Acute pancreatitis (inflammation of the pancreas)
E015. Chronic pancreatitis (inflammation of the pancreas)

Gastrointestinal tract - small intestine and large intestine
E016. Acute obstipation (constipation)
E017. Chronic obstipation (constipation)
E018. Colon irritabile
E019. Diverticulitis
E020. Acquired lactose intolerance (lactose malabsorption)
E021. Fructose malabsorption
E022. Glutensensitive enteropathy (celiac disease)
E023. Colectomy
E024. Short Bowel Syndrome

Gastrointestinal tract - liver, gallbladder, bile ducts
E025. Acute and chronic hepatitis (inflammation of the liver)
E026. Cholelithiasis (bile stones)
E027. fatty liver
E028. cirrhosis

Gastrointestinal tract - Stomach and duodenal intestine
E029. Acute gastritis
E030. Chronic gastritis
E031. Stomach bleeding
E032. Ulcus ventriculi and duodenal ulcer
E033. Condition after gastric surgery

Gastrointestinal tract - oral cavity and esophagus
E034. Stomatitis
E035. Esophageal carcinoma (esophageal cancer)
E036. Refluosophagitis (heartburn)

Special diseases
E037. Phenylketonuria (PKU)
E038. Rheumatic joint diseases

Metabolism
E039. Obesity (overweight)
E040. Diabetes mellitus
E041. Eating disorders (underweight)

Fat metabolism
E042. Hypercholesterolaemia (increased cholesterol level)
E043. Hepatic Encephalopathy

Heart and circulation
E044. Arteriosclerosis (arterial calcification)
E045. Heart insufficiency
E046. Hypertension
E047. Hyperuricaemia and gout

Changed nutrient requirements
E048. In case of fever
E049. For malignant diseases
E050. After burns
E051. Radiation and chemotherapy

CANCER
E100. Pancreatic cancer
E101. Bladder cancer
E102. Blood cancer (leukemia)
E103. Breast cancer
E104. Colorectal cancer
E105. Gastric cancer
E106. Kidney cancer
E107. Esophageal cancer

TCM
E200. Bladder - moisture heat in the bladder
E201. Bladder - moisture and cold in the bladder
E202. Bladder - emptiness and cold in the bladder
E203. Large intestine - external cold affects the large intestine
E204. Large intestine - moisture heat in the large intestine
E205. Large intestine - heat blocks the intestine II acute
E206. Large intestine - dryness of the colon
E207. Large intestine - Yang deficiency (cold)
E208. Heart - Blood insufficiency
E209. Heart - Blood stagnation
E210. Heart - Fire
E211. Heart - Hot mucus clogs the heart pores

E212. Heart - Cold mucus clogs the heart pores
E213. Heart - Qi deficiency
E214. Heart - Yang deficiency
E215. Heart - Yin deficiency
E216. Liver - Ascending Liver Yang
E217. Liver - Blood deficiency
E218. Liver - Blood stagnation
E219. Liver - Moisture heat in liver and gall bladder
E220. Liver - Fire
E221. Liver - Gall bladder Qi-Empty
E222. Liver - Cold in the liver meridian
E223. Liver - Qi stagnation
E224. Liver - Wind
E225. Liver - Wind with ascending liver Yang
E226. Liver - Wind with blood anemic
E227. Liver - Wind with extreme heat
E228. Lung - Qi deficiency
E229. Lung - Mucus-moisture in the lungs
E230. Lung - Mucus-heat in the lungs
E231. Lung - Mucus-cold in the lungs
E232. Lung - Dryness of the lungs
E233. Lung - Wind-heat attacks the lungs
E234. Lung - Wind-cold affects the lungs
E235. Lung - Yin deficiency
E236. Stomach - Bloodstagnation
E237. Stomach - Fire
E238. Stomach - Cold with liquid
E239. Stomach - Nutrition stagnation
E240. Stomach - Qi deficiency
E241. Stomach - Rebellious Qi
E242. Stomach - Yin Emptiness
E243. Spleen - Heat and moisture attack the spleen
E244. Spleen - Coldness and moisture affects the spleen
E245. Spleen - Qi deficiency
E246. Spleen - Qi deficiency + Declining spleen Qi
E247. Spleen - Qi deficiency + spleen does not control the blood
E248. Spleen - Yang deficiency
E249. Kidney - Heart and kidney no longer communicate
E250. Kidney - Jing deficiency
E251. Kidney - Kidneys cannot receive the Qi
E252. Kidney - Qi is not stable
E253. Kidney - Yang deficiency
E254. Kidney - Yin deficiency

For further information visit di-book.com.